DISCARD

TINY DOGS

POMERANIANS

by Allan Morey

Consultant: Jennifer Zablotny
Doctor of Veterinary Medicine
American Veterinary
Medical Association

Pebble® Plus

CAPSTONE PRESS
a capstone imprint

Pebble Plus is published by Capstone Press,
1710 Roe Crest Drive, North Mankato, Minnesota 56003
www.mycapstone.com

Library of Congress Cataloging-in-Publication Data
Names: Morey, Allan, author.
Title: Pomeranians / by Allen Morey.
Description: North Mankato, Minnesota : Capstone Press, [2017] | Series:
   Pebble plus. Tiny dogs | Includes bibliographical references and index.
Identifiers: LCCN 2016006875| ISBN 9781515719670 (library binding) | ISBN
   9781515719731 (ebook (pdf))
Subjects: LCSH: Pomeranian dog—Juvenile literature. | Toy dogs—Juvenile
   literature.
Classification: LCC SF429.P8 M68 2017 | DDC 636.76—dc23
LC record available at https://lccn.loc.gov/2016006875

Editorial Credits
Emily Raij, editor; Juliette Peters, designer;
Pam Mitsakos, media researcher; Laura Manthe, production specialist

Photo Credits
iStockphoto: anurakpong, 10–11; Shutterstock: DRHUTCH, 14–15, InBetweentheBlinks, 1,
kostolom3000, 3, back cover top left, KPG Payless2, 7, Liliya Kulianionak, cover, Michelle D. Milliman,
13, mikumistock, 17, Noiz Stocker, 19, stockphoto mania, 21, Suponev Vladimir, 9, vlastas, design
element throughout book, Vtls, 5

Note to Parents and Teachers

The Tiny Dogs set supports national science standards related to life science. This book describes
and illustrates Pomeranians. The images support early readers in understanding the text. The
repetition of words and phrases helps early readers learn new words. This book also introduces
early readers to subject-specific vocabulary words, which are defined in the Glossary section. Early
readers may need assistance to read some words and to use the Table of Contents, Glossary, Read
More, Internet Sites, Critical Thinking Using the Common Core, and Index sections of the book.

Printed in the United States of America.
009656F16

TABLE OF CONTENTS

PUFFBALLS

Do you like fluffy dogs?
Pomeranians have two layers
of fluffy fur. Their bushy tails lie
on their backs. People call these
dogs Poms for short.

Poms were bred from sled dogs.

They lived in cold places.

That is why they have thick fur.

Today these little dogs make

loving pets.

LITTLE AND LOUD

A pom is about the size and weight of a housecat. Poms are small enough to fit in your lap. But their personalities are big!

A pom's coat can be almost

any color or pattern.

Many have orange, red, or tan fur.

Some are white with patches

of another color.

These little dogs have a lot of
energy. They love to run and play.
Poms need owners who take them
on walks every day.
Healthy poms can live 15 years.

Poms are barkers. They yip
at other dogs and people.
They yap at strange sounds.
Poms need training to learn
when not to bark.

POMS AS PETS

Poms' coats need grooming. They should be brushed a few times a week. This gets out knots. Poms do not need baths often.

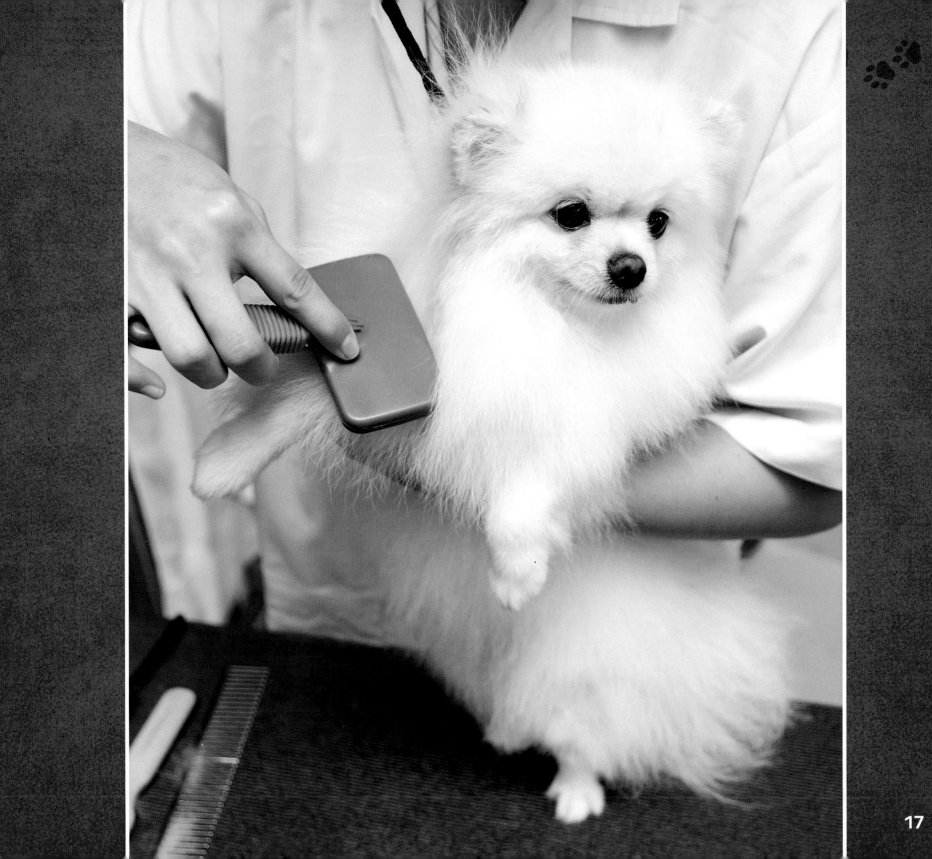

Little poms make great watchdogs.

They are protective of their family.

They bark to let you know

someone is near.

Poms need to be around people.

They are loyal pets.

They might misbehave if left alone.

Luckily, they are easy to take

with you!

GLOSSARY

bark—the short, loud sound a dog makes

breed—to mate and produce young

coat—an animal's hair or fur

groom—to clean and make an animal look neat

loyal—being true to something or someone

protective—guarding or keeping safe from harm

train—to prepare for something by learning or practicing new skills

READ MORE

Green, Sara. *Pomeranians.* Dog Breeds. Minneapolis: Bellwether Media, 2011.

Landau, Elaine. *Pomeranians Are the Best!* Best Dogs Ever. Minneapolis: Lerner, 2011.

Shores, Erika L. *Pet Dogs up Close.* Pets Up Close. North Mankato, Minn.: Capstone Press, 2014.

INTERNET SITES

FactHound offers a safe, fun way to find Internet sites related to this book. All of the sites on FactHound have been researched by our staff.

Here's all you do:

Visit *www.facthound.com*

Type in this code: 9781515719670

 **Super-cool stuff!** Check out projects, games and lots more at
www.capstonekids.com

CRITICAL THINKING USING THE COMMON CORE

1. Pomeranians were bred from sledding dogs. What traits do you think sled dogs need to live in the cold and pull a sled? (Integration of Knowledge and Ideas)

2. What would be the most difficult thing about having a Pomeranian for a pet? Why? (Integration of Knowledge and Ideas)

3. Name two colors that Pomeranians can be. (Key Ideas and Details)

INDEX